Herbes de Provence

Herbes de Provence

COOKING WITH THE HERBS OF SOUTHERN FRANCE

ethel w. brennan

ILLUSTRATIONS BY diane bigda

CHRONICLE BOOKS

SAN FRANCISCO

LIBRARY OF CONGRESS CATALOGING-IN-PUBLICATION DATA:

Brennan, Ethel.
    Herbes de Provence / by Ethel W. Brennan.
    p.   cm. — (The artful kitchen series)
    Includes index.
    ISBN 0-8118-1933-7
    1. Cookery (Herbs)   2. Cookery, French—Provençal style.
3. Herbs—France—Provence. I. Title. II. Series.
TX819.H4B698   1999
641.6'57—dc21   97-47107
                     CIP

Printed in Singapore.

BOOK DESIGN BY Julia Flagg

The illustrator wishes to thank her husband, Doug, and her mother, Phyllis.

Distributed in Canada by Raincoast Books
8680 Cambie Street
Vancouver, British Columbia V6P 6M9

10 9 8 7 6 5 4 3 2 1

Chronicle Books
85 Second Street
San Francisco, California 94105

Web Site: www.chroniclebooks.com

I dedicate this little book to my four parents,

Mom and Jim

and

Dad and Aura,

who have supported me endlessly through all my projects.

I love you, Ethel.

ACKNOWLEDGMENTS

I would like to thank Bill LeBlond and Leslie Jonath for thinking of me for this book, and especially Leslie for all of her encouragement. I would also like to thank Sarah Putman and Mikyla Bruder for their help and editing. Thank you to Sharon Silva who has taught me so much over the years and is a wonderful editor. Thank you to my dear friend Rachel Shiffman for testing these recipes, and thank you to Laurent Rigobert (who I am crazy about) for eating them, and finally to my mom, Georgeanne Brennan, who is always available, supportive, encouraging, and wonderful, thank you.

Fresh Provençal Herbs

Dried Herbes de Provence Blends

I spent much of my childhood in a four-hundred-year-old farmhouse in the rocky foothills of Haute Provence. My parents raised goats and used the milk for making cheeses that we sold at local markets. Our neighbors were a collection of farmers, village officials (our village had only two hundred people), and artisans. In the evenings, everyone would get together over glasses of pastis and rosé and talk of the best melons to cultivate or of gossip at the mayor's office.

What I remember most from those days, and of the summers I later spent in that house, is the food, which I see as defined largely by the use of herbs. Indeed, Provence is perfumed from its landscape to its kitchens with the fragrance of rosemary, sage, thyme, juniper, winter savory, lavender, and bay.

Herbes de Provence, a dried herb mixture sold in small ceramic or clay pots throughout the region, is known by cooks far beyond the borders of the province. It is usually made by mixing together four or five of the area's most abundant herbs. Many Provençal cooks argue that these mixes combine far too many elements, resulting in musty blends that are an anathema to good food, and that lavender in particular is for soaps and perfumes and not for eating. But I feel that if you dry your own herbs and make your own mixtures, the results will enhance your dishes, and that even lavender has a place at the table.

In my kitchen, an informal herbes de Provence mixture is always on hand. Whenever I pick or buy fresh herbs, I toss some of the loose sprigs into a shallow basket on the counter, where they dry nicely. Then when I am cooking, I crumble together an assortment and add them into a marinade, sauce, soup, or stew. Sometimes I crush a ribbon or two of dried lemon or orange zest as well, flavors that also play important roles in the Provençal pantry.

The culinary properties of fresh and dried herbs are, of course, very different, and the use of the two should not be considered interchangeable. In general, as herbs dry, the essential oils lose their intensity and the herbs tend to sweeten or mellow. Sage, for example, is quite pungent when fresh, but much of its bitterness diminishes as it dries, while mint becomes much sweeter.

This small volume is divided into two parts. The first section is a collection of recipes that individually showcase the herbs that grow abundantly throughout Provence: bay, fennel, juniper, lavender, rosemary, sage, thyme, and winter savory. Brief descriptions of the herbs open the section, and the recipes emphasize using them fresh. The second section contains recipes flavored with the famed dried herbes de Provence. It provides directions for drying herbs and for making three outstanding mixes.

Fresh Provençal Herbs

Shelling Beans and Sage Salad

Roasted Pork Loin with Fresh Sage and Morel Mushrooms

Roasted Chicken Stuffed with Sage

Haricots Verts Salad with Thyme

Orange and Fennel Salad with Thyme Vinaigrette

Baked Trout with Lemon and Thyme

Blackberry Jam with Lemon Zest and Lemon Thyme

Tomato and Corn Chowder

Rosemary Spice Cake

Smelt Grilled with Rosemary

Caramelized Pearl Onions with Lavender

Pear and Lavender Tarte Tatin

Chocolate Lavender Cake

Carrot Soup with Winter Savory and Garlic Crostini

Bulgur Wheat with Fennel and Parsley

Wild Mushroom and Juniper Berry Sandwiches

Fresh Provençal Herbs Although a number of herbs—including basil, chervil, chives, oregano, parsley, and sweet marjoram—are widely used in Provençal cooking, there are certain hardy perennials that especially thrive in this rugged landscape, with its blazing sun and poor but well-drained soil. The herbs described here are those native herbs that flourish in Provence. A trip through Provence, from the dry coastal areas through the rich valleys of the Rhône River and into the high desert plains, leaves the traveler with memories of blue skies and air heavy with the fragrances of the local kitchen. The name of each herb is rendered in English, French, and the unique dialect of Provence.

Bay Laurel ≈ *Le Laurier* ≈ **Lou Lausie**

This tree, which has been nicknamed the Queen of Provençal Cooking, produces aromatic leaves considered essential to the seasoning of many sauces and stews and to the classic bouquet garni. The leaves are sometimes speared along with chunks of meat onto skewers for grilling, or, in the past, were twisted into crowns for rewarding diligent schoolchildren. Bay complements rich tomato- and wine-based stews and sauces, red meats, and game.

Fennel ≈ *Le Fenouil* ≈ **Lou Fenou**

This herb, with its intriguing anise flavor, grows abundantly along the roadsides of Provence. The fernlike tops and dried seeds are used to season stocks and fish dishes. The seeds are also a fragrant addition to dried herb mixtures.

Juniper ～ Le Genièvre ～ Lou Marrit Cade

This prickly shrub, found on hillsides and in valleys, is considered the perfect seasoning for wild fowl and game, terrines, and pâtés. The oils present in the shrub's small, dark berries deliver a pungent bouquet.

Lavender ～ La Lavande ～ La Lavandou

This herb is native to Provence and grows wild throughout much of the region. It has also been widely cultivated for nearly a century to meet commercial demand, and nowadays vivid purple fields blanket the high plateaus of Provence during July and August. Lavender has a strong flavor whether fresh or dried, and can easily overpower a dish if not used judiciously. The blossoms, stems, and leaves can all be used in cooking, especially in cakes and tarts, with the flowers carrying the most intense flavor.

Rosemary ⁓ *Le Romarain* ⁓ **Lou Roumanieu**

This tall bush, often found in the sunny corner of a Provençal garden, symbolizes remembrance and is historically incorporated into local wedding ceremonies. Although its flavor is quite strong, making it suitable for pairing with lamb or earthy vegetables such as mushrooms and winter squashes, it possesses a hint of sweetness that complements some desserts and baked goods.

Sage ⁓ *La Sauge* ⁓ **La Sauvio**

This herb flourishes on the high prairies. Its beautiful purple flowers subtly mimic the flavor of its gray-green leaves, and a sweet nectar collects at the base of each blossom. Use the flower to accent salads or in place of the leaves in cooking. Sage marries well with meats, especially pork, and is often used in baking savory breads or puddings.

Thyme ~ *Le Thym* ~ **Lou Farigoulo**

Thyme is indispensable to the Provençal cook, virtually defining the culinary character of the region. Its most common companion is bay, and the two are essential for making a bouquet garni. Several thyme varieties are in the markets, including French, lemon, silver, and English, and each has its distinctive flavor. Wild thyme *(le serpolet or la farigouleto)* grows in the high mountains, where sheep and goats happily graze on it. It tends to have a milder aroma but a more bitter taste than its cultivated kin. Thyme is a wonderful seasoning for wild mushrooms such as chanterelles or morels, or even for their more common cultivated relatives.

Winter Savory ~ *La Sariette* ~ **Pebre d'Aï**

Very similar to thyme in its flavor, this herb also has hints of pepper and mint. It can turn up in a bouquet garni and is used to season many foods, from goat cheeses to vegetable dishes.

LA SAUGE

Shelling Beans and Sage Salad

Shelling beans appear in the markets of Provence in late summer and early fall, when they are flourishing in farmers' fields. This salad, with its generous measure of sage, accentuates the light flavor and tenderness of the beans.

3 quarts water
1 yellow onion, quartered
1 1/4 teaspoons salt
3 cups shelled cranberry or flageolet beans
    (about 2 pounds unshelled)
2 tablespoons extra-virgin olive oil
2 teaspoons red wine vinegar
1 teaspoon freshly ground black pepper
2 tablespoons finely chopped fresh sage
1/2 cup quartered cherry tomatoes such as
    Sweet 100s or other flavorful varieties

In a large saucepan, bring the water to a boil. Add the onion and 1 teaspoon of the salt, and let boil for 5 minutes. Add the beans and cook until tender, about 10 minutes. Drain into a colander and immediately place under cold running water for at least 1 minute to halt the cooking.

In a bowl, whisk together the olive oil, vinegar, the remaining 1/4 teaspoon salt, the pepper, and the sage. Add the beans and tomatoes and toss until well coated with the vinaigrette. Transfer to a serving dish and serve at room temperature or chilled.

SERVES 4.

Roasted Pork Loin with Fresh Sage and Morel Mushrooms

⋘ Here, the classic combination of sage and pork is broadened with the addition of honeycombed morels. When the roast is sliced, it reveals a spiral of the sweet herb and earthy mushrooms that perfume the pork.

1 boneless pork loin, about 1 $^1\!/_2$ pounds, butterflied

$^1\!/_4$ pound fresh morel mushrooms, brushed clean (or rinsed if very dirty) and finely chopped, *or* $^1\!/_2$ ounce dried morel mushrooms soaked in $^1\!/_2$ cup boiling water for 20 minutes, drained, and finely chopped

$^1\!/_4$ cup finely chopped fresh sage

1 clove garlic, peeled and minced

$^1\!/_2$ teaspoon salt

1 teaspoon freshly ground black pepper

2 tablespoons olive oil

1 yellow onion, quartered and then thinly sliced

$^1\!/_2$ cup dry white wine

$^1\!/_4$ cup water, or as needed

Lay the pork loin out flat, as if an opened book. In a small bowl, combine the mushrooms, sage, garlic, $^1\!/_4$ teaspoon of the salt, and $^1\!/_2$ teaspoon of the pepper. Mix well and spread evenly over the pork. Starting from a long side, roll the pork loin into a cylinder, and tie at 2- or 3-inch intervals with kitchen string. Rub the remaining $^1\!/_4$ teaspoon salt and $^1\!/_2$ teaspoon pepper over the surface of the pork loin. Wrap tightly in plastic wrap and refrigerate for at least 1 hour or for up to 24 hours.

Preheat an oven to 375 degrees F.

In a flameproof baking dish or deep skillet with a lid, warm the olive oil over medium heat. Add the onion slices and sauté until they begin to brown, about 7 minutes. Add the pork loin and sear well on all sides, 3 to 4 minutes. Pour in the white wine and deglaze the dish, scraping up any browned bits.

Cover with the lid and transfer to the oven. Cook, basting every 10 to 15 minutes and adding the water a tablespoon or so at a time if the pan becomes too dry, until the pork loin is firm to the touch and the juices run clear when it is pierced, 40 to 45 minutes. Transfer to a serving platter, let stand for a few minutes, and cut into thin slices. Serve immediately.

SERVES 4.

NOTE: It's best to choose a pan in which the pork loin fits somewhat snugly (1 to 2 inches of space around the meat). This way, more natural juices are retained and less additional water is needed.

Roasted Chicken Stuffed with Sage

Crispy skin and tender, succulent flesh are the hallmarks of properly roasted chicken. The sage permeates the chicken during roasting and seasons it throughout. Pass Dijon mustard at the table, as is the custom in France.

1 chicken, about 3 pounds
1 teaspoon olive oil
$\frac{1}{2}$ teaspoon salt
1 teaspoon freshly ground black pepper
2 bunches fresh sage
4 cloves garlic, peeled but left whole

Preheat an oven to 400 degrees F.

Rinse the chicken inside and out and pat dry. Rub the chicken all over with the olive oil, salt, and pepper. Separate 4 large leaves from the sage bunches. Place the chicken in a roasting pan, breast side up. Using your fingertips, gently separate the skin from the breast meat and slip 2 of the sage leaves, about 1 inch apart, between the skin and the meat on each breast half. Fill the cavity with the remaining sage and the garlic cloves.

Roast, uncovered, basting with the pan juices every 10 to 15 minutes, until golden brown and the juices run clear when a knife is inserted deep into the thigh joint, 50 to 60 minutes. Transfer to a platter and let stand for a few minutes, then carve and serve.

SERVES 4.

Haricots Verts Salad with Thyme

Haricots verts, also called French fillet beans, are very slender green beans that have not yet begun to develop seeds and are therefore tender and meaty. In this dish, they are barely cooked so that they retain their crunch and are then tossed with fragrant olive oil and fresh herbs.

4 quarts water

1 $^1/_4$ teaspoons salt

1 $^1/_4$ pounds (about 4 cups) haricots verts,
    stem ends trimmed

2 tablespoons extra-virgin olive oil

2 teaspoons red wine vinegar

$^1/_2$ teaspoon freshly ground black pepper

$^1/_2$ teaspoon salt

$^1/_2$ clove garlic, peeled and minced

1 tablespoon finely chopped fresh Italian parsley

1 teaspoon finely chopped fresh thyme

In a large saucepan, bring the water to a boil. Add 1 teaspoon of the salt and the haricots verts and boil until just tender but still crunchy, 4 to 6 minutes. Drain into a colander and immediately place under cold running water for 30 to 40 seconds to halt the cooking.

In a bowl, whisk together the olive oil, vinegar, pepper, the remaining $^1/_4$ teaspoon salt, garlic, parsley, and thyme. Add the slightly warm beans and turn until well coated. Transfer to a serving dish and serve barely warm or at room temperature.

SERVES 4.

Orange and Fennel Salad with Thyme Vinaigrette

During the cool-weather months, this flavorful combination makes an elegant presentation. Trimmed fennel bulbs, like cut apples, artichokes, and pears, discolor when exposed to air, so it is important to coat lightly with lemon juice.

2 fennel bulbs
$1/2$ lemon
2 navel oranges
2 tablespoons extra-virgin olive oil
2 teaspoons balsamic vinegar
$1/4$ teaspoon salt
$1/2$ teaspoon freshly ground black pepper
2 teaspoons finely chopped fresh thyme
$1/4$ cup slivered blanched almonds, toasted

Cut off the stems and feathery tops from the fennel bulbs and reserve for another use. Trim away any bruised or otherwise damaged stalks. Cut away the tough cores and cut crosswise into $1/8$-inch-thick slices. Place in a bowl and squeeze on the lemon juice from the lemon half. Turn to coat and set aside.

Working with 1 orange at a time, cut a thick slice off the top and bottom. Then, holding the orange upright, cut off the peel and all the white membrane. Cut the oranges crosswise into $1/4$-inch-thick slices.

In a good-sized bowl, whisk together the olive oil, vinegar, salt, pepper, and thyme. Using a slotted spoon, transfer the fennel to the bowl. Add the orange slices and gently toss together to coat evenly. Beginning with the oranges, arrange the slices on a serving platter. Transfer the fennel slices, piling them on top of the orange slices. Sprinkle with the almonds and serve at room temperature.

SERVES 4.

Baked Trout with Lemon and Thyme

Trout are a favorite river fish of Provence, especially in the higher altitudes far from the Mediterranean. Restaurants often boast tanks of live trout, ready for cooking in a wood-fired oven.

2 trout, 14 to 16 ounces each, cleaned
2 teaspoons olive oil
1 bunch fresh thyme
2 lemons
1/2 teaspoon salt
1 teaspoon freshly ground black pepper

Preheat an oven to 325 degrees F.

Rub the trout all over with the olive oil. Place them, bellies facing each other and tails at opposite ends, in a shallow baking dish. Fill each fish cavity with an equal amount of the thyme. Cut 1 lemon into 1/4-inch-thick slices, and slip in as many slices as will fit on top of each bed of thyme. Tuck any remaining lemon slices between or around the fish. Sprinkle the trout with the salt and pepper.

Place in the oven and bake, uncovered, until the flesh is firm and white, about 20 minutes. Remove from the oven. Cut the remaining lemon into wedges and serve with the trout.

SERVES 4.

Blackberry Jam with Lemon Zest and Lemon Thyme

This recipe can also be made with raspberries, peaches, or apricots. The use of the lemon thyme and lemon zest adds a faint tanginess to the sweet, fruity jam.

1 lemon
4 quarts plus 1 cup water
2 cups sugar
4 pints (8 cups) fresh blackberries
3 fresh lemon thyme sprigs

Using a paring knife, cut 3 strips of zest from the lemon, each 2 inches long and $\frac{1}{2}$ inch wide. Try not to get too much of the white pith, although a little is fine since it acts as a natural pectin. Cut the zest strips lengthwise into very narrow pieces, and then cut crosswise into $\frac{1}{2}$-inch-long pieces. Set aside.

In a heavy saucepan, bring the 1 cup water to a boil and stir in the sugar. Cook, stirring constantly, until the sugar is dissolved, about 2 minutes. Add the berries, lemon zest, and lemon thyme. Bring to a boil and cook for 5 minutes, then reduce the heat to low. Cook, stirring often and regularly skimming any foam that develops on the surface, until the jam is thick but not solid and easily adheres to the back of a spoon, about 40 minutes.

Just before the jam is ready, in a large saucepan, bring the 4 quarts water to a boil. Slip two 1-pint and one $\frac{1}{2}$-pint canning jars and their lids into the water and boil for 2 to 3 minutes to sterilize. Using tongs, remove the jars, lids, and rings, draining well.

When the jam is done, remove and discard the thyme sprigs. Spoon the hot jam into the dry, hot sterilized jars, filling them to within $\frac{1}{4}$ inch of the rims. Wipe the rims clean, place a lid atop each jar, and seal with the screw bands. Let stand until cool.

Press down on each lid; if it remains depressed, the seal is good and the jam can be stored in a cool, dry place for up to 6 months. If the lid pops up, the seal has failed; store in the refrigerator for up to 2 weeks.

MAKES 2 $\frac{1}{2}$ PINTS.

Tomato and Corn Chowder

This soup is a simple tribute to the produce of summer. It marries the flavors of ripe, mildly acidic tomatoes and sweet corn, tied together with the distinctive taste of fresh rosemary.

4 cups water
2 pounds ripe tomatoes
2 tablespoons olive oil
$1/2$ cup finely chopped yellow onion
Kernels cut from 2 ears corn
2 tablespoons minced fresh rosemary
2 cloves garlic, peeled and minced
$1/2$ teaspoon pepper
$1/4$ teaspoon salt
2 cups vegetable or chicken stock
$1/2$ cup milk, preferably whole
4 teaspoons heavy cream

In a saucepan, bring the water to a boil. Add the tomatoes and leave for 30 seconds, then remove. Allow the tomatoes to cool slightly, gently remove the skins, the cores, and stem ends. Chop coarsely, capturing the juice, and set aside.

In a large saucepan over medium heat, warm the olive oil. Add the onion and sauté until tender, about 5 minutes. Add the corn, rosemary, and garlic and sauté for another 2 minutes. Stir in the tomatoes and their juices and cook for about 5 minutes. Pour in the stock, add salt and pepper, and bring to a boil. Reduce the heat to low and simmer, uncovered, until the soup has thickened slightly and the corn is tender, 15 to 20 minutes.

Stir in the milk and cook gently for 2 minutes. Remove from the heat and serve, swirling 1 teaspoon cream onto the top of each serving.

SERVES 4.

Rosemary Spice Cake

Aromatic and moist, this cake derives its richness from the combination of sweet fruit and squash, spices and fresh rosemary. Serve with a smoky English tea.

1 cup water
1 small zucchini, grated
1 large sweet apple, peeled, cored, and
    cut into a $^1/_2$-inch dice
1 cup sugar
7 tablespoons margarine
1 tablespoon minced fresh rosemary
$^1/_2$ teaspoon salt
$^1/_2$ teaspoon freshly grated nutmeg
$^1/_4$ teaspoon ground cloves
2 cups all-purpose flour
1 teaspoon baking powder
1 teaspoon baking soda

Preheat an oven to 325 degrees F. Grease a 9-inch round or square cake pan.

In a saucepan, combine the water, zucchini, apple, sugar, margarine, rosemary, salt, nutmeg, and cloves. Bring to a boil over medium heat, stirring occasionally, and cook for 1 to 2 minutes. Remove from the heat and let cool completely.

Meanwhile, in a large bowl, sift together the flour, baking powder, and baking soda. Gently stir the cooled zucchini mixture into the flour mixture just until mixed. Pour into the prepared cake pan.

Bake until a knife inserted into the center comes out clean, 35 to 40 minutes. Transfer to a rack to cool, then turn out onto a serving plate or serve directly from the pan.

SERVES 6 TO 9.

Smelt Grilled with Rosemary

Until the mid-1970s, a caravan of fish, bread, and butcher shop trucks would roll into the villages of Provence, come to a stop, the sides of the trucks would open, and the drivers would sell the freshest and most flavorful products to the residents. The fish truck was my favorite, and I always requested the tiny smelt. The fact that one could eat the little fish whole delighted me.

1 pound smelt (whitebait), cleaned
4 teaspoons extra-virgin olive oil
1 teaspoon salt
1 teaspoon freshly ground black pepper
12 fresh rosemary sprigs
1 lemon, cut into 4 wedges

Prepare a fire in a charcoal grill.

Divide the smelt into 4 equal portions. Place each portion in the center of a 10-inch square of aluminum foil, arranging the fish in a single layer. Drizzle each portion with 1 teaspoon of the olive oil, sprinkle evenly with the salt and pepper, and lay 3 rosemary sprigs atop each serving of fish. Fold up the edges, creating 4 shallow pans with 1-inch rims.

Place the pans on the grill rack and grill until the fish are opaque throughout, 7 to 10 minutes.

Slip the fish onto individual plates and garnish with the lemon wedges. Serve at once.

SERVES 4.

Caramelized Pearl Onions with Lavender

These tiny onions turn golden brown and are faintly flavored with the lavender blossoms. Serve with grilled pork chops and mashed potatoes.

1 ½ pounds (2 cups) pearl onions
2 tablespoons unsalted butter
½ teaspoon brown sugar
2 tablespoons cider vinegar
½ teaspoon fresh lavender blossoms or 1 teaspoon dried blossoms
⅓ cup water, or as needed

Bring a saucepan of water to a boil. Add the onions and boil for 2 to 3 minutes. Drain and immediately place under cold running water to cool. Cut off the root ends and the stem ends, if desired, and slip off the skins.

In a large skillet over high heat, melt the butter. When it begins to foam, add the onions. Cook, stirring occasionally, until the onions begin to soften and brown, 3 to 5 minutes. Add the sugar, vinegar, and lavender blossoms and reduce the heat to medium. Continue to cook, stirring often and adding the water a tablespoon at a time if the onions begin to stick, until the onions are tender and can easily be pierced with a knife, about 25 to 30 minutes.

Transfer the onions to a serving dish and serve hot.

SERVES 6 TO 8.

Pear and Lavender Tarte Tatin

Here, the famed French upside-down apple tart is given a new look and taste with the use of pears and fragrant lavender.

FOR THE PASTRY:

1 cup plus 2 tablespoons all-purpose
   flour

1 teaspoon sugar

6 ¹/₂ tablespoons unsalted butter,
   cut into pieces

About 3 tablespoons ice water

FOR THE FILLING:

¹/₃ cup brandy

2 tablespoons brown sugar

1 teaspoon fresh or dried lavender blossoms

3 Bartlett pears, peeled, halved, cored, and cut
   lengthwise into ¹/₄-inch-thick slices

1 ¹/₂ teaspoons unsalted butter, cut into bits

TO MAKE THE PASTRY: In a food processor, combine 1 cup of the flour and the sugar and pulse once or twice to mix. Add the butter and process until the mixture has the texture of coarse cornmeal. Add the ice water 1 tablespoon at a time and process just until the dough comes together in a rough mass. Remove from the processor, form into a ball, wrap in plastic wrap, and chill for about 15 minutes.

MEANWHILE, MAKE THE FILLING: In a large bowl, stir together the brandy, brown sugar, and lavender blossoms. Gently fold in the pears, coating them well with the brandy mixture. Let stand for 15 to 20 minutes.

Preheat an oven to 375 degrees F. Butter the bottom and sides of a 9-inch round shallow pie dish.

Dust a work surface with the remaining 2 tablespoons flour. Roll out the pastry into a round 11 to 12 inches in diameter.

Arrange the pear slices in the prepared dish in three layers, forming concentric circles on each layer and slightly overlapping the slices. Pour the brandy-lavender mixture remaining in the bowl evenly over the pears. Dot the pears with the butter. Working carefully, cover the pears with the pastry round. Tuck the pastry overhang inside the pie dish, pressing it against the inner edge to create a fitted, inverted crust. Prick the crust in several places with the tines of a fork.

Bake until the crust is golden and the juices are bubbling at the edges of the dish, 35 to 40 minutes. Remove from the oven and let cool slightly, about 10 minutes. Invert a serving plate over the tart and then quickly invert together. Lift off the pie dish. Serve immediately.

SERVES 6.

Chocolate Lavender Cake

Lightly perfumed with lavender, this dense chocolate cake is quick to prepare and makes an impressive presentation.

4 eggs, separated
$^1/_4$ teaspoon salt
8 ounces semisweet chocolate, broken into 1-inch pieces
3 tablespoons Amarone wine, brandy, or Marsala
8 tablespoons (1 stick) unsalted butter, cut into $^1/_2$-inch pieces
2 tablespoons granulated sugar
1 teaspoon finely crushed dried lavender blossoms
$^1/_2$ cup sifted all-purpose flour
$^1/_2$ pint (1 cup) raspberries
1 teaspoon confectioners' sugar

Preheat an oven to 375 degrees F. Butter and flour the bottom and sides of a 9-inch springform cake pan.

In a small bowl, whisk the egg yolks until well blended. In a separate bowl, add the salt to the egg whites and, using an electric mixer, beat to form stiff peaks.

In a medium saucepan over low heat, combine the chocolate, 2 tablespoons of the wine, butter, granulated sugar, and lavender. Heat, stirring constantly, until the chocolate is completely melted and the mixture is well blended. Remove from the heat and let cool for 30 seconds. Slowly pour in the egg yolks, whisking constantly until well blended. Add the flour in 3 batches, stirring until blended. The texture will not be smooth. Using a rubber spatula, fold the egg whites, in three batches, into the chocolate mixture.

Pour the batter into the prepared cake pan. Bake until a knife inserted into the center comes out clean, about 25 minutes. The cake will have puffed up but will fall promptly upon removal from the oven.

While the cake is cooking, combine the raspberries and the remaining wine and let stand.

Let cool for about 10 minutes, then release the pan sides. Slide the cake onto a serving plate. Let cool completely. Using a slotted spoon, remove the berries from the wine and arrange them atop the cake. Sift the confectioners' sugar over the top.

SERVES 12.

Carrot Soup with Winter Savory and Garlic Crostini

Sweet carrots seasoned with pungent winter savory are an ideal combination for a simple soup.

FOR THE CROSTINI:
8 baguette slices, each $1/2$ inch thick
1 clove garlic, peeled
1 teaspoon olive oil

FOR THE SOUP:
1 tablepoon olive oil
$1/2$ cup finely chopped yellow onion
1 clove garlic, peeled and minced
1 tablespoon minced winter savory
$1/2$ teaspoon salt
1 teaspoon freshly ground black pepper
1 stalk celery, finely chopped
4 medium carrots, peeled, quartered lengthwise,
     and sliced crosswise into $1/2$-inch-thick pieces
2 cups water and 2 cups vegetable broth
4 teaspoons freshly grated Parmesan cheese

Preheat an oven to 425 degrees F.

TO MAKE THE CROSTINI: Rub each baguette slice on both sides with the garlic clove. Drizzle the olive oil evenly over the slices. Place on a baking sheet and toast in the oven, turning once, until lightly golden, about 7 to 10 minutes total. Set aside.

TO MAKE THE SOUP: In a large saucepan over medium heat, warm the olive oil. Add the onion, garlic, savory, salt, and pepper. Cook, stirring often, until the onion is soft, 3 to 5 minutes. Stir in the celery and cook for another minute, just to release its water. Add the carrots and turn to coat evenly with the oil. Pour in 1 cup of the water and stir to scrape any browned bits from the pan bottom. Bring to a boil and add the remaining 3 cups water. Return to a boil, reduce the heat to low, cover, and simmer until the carrots are soft, about 35 to 40 minutes. Remove from the heat and let cool slightly. Working in 1-cup batches, purée in a food processor or blender. Ladle into warmed bowls and top each serving with 2 crostini and 1 teaspoon of the cheese. Serve immediately.

SERVES 4.

PARMESAN

LA SARIETTE

Bulgur Wheat with Fennel and Parsley

Bulgur wheat has a wonderful, light, fluffy texture that blends well with other ingredients. In this case, a mix of crushed fennel seeds and the feathery leaves is married with the grain.

²/₃ cup bulgur wheat
1 ½ cups boiling water
¼ cup finely chopped Italian parsley leaves
¼ cup finely chopped fennel leaves
1 clove garlic, peeled and finely chopped
¼ cup finely chopped red onion
2 tablespoons freshly squeezed lemon juice
1 tablespoon extra-virgin olive oil
¼ teaspoon salt
Whole black peppercorns
½ teaspoon fennel seeds, lightly crushed

Place the bulgur wheat in a heatproof bowl, add the boiling water, and let stand for 30 minutes. Drain well, pressing out excess moisture.

In a large salad bowl, mix bulgur, parsley, fennel leaves, garlic, red onion, and lemon juice.

With a mortar and pestle, crush together salt, peppercorns, and fennel seeds. Add this mixture to the bulgur along with the olive oil and toss together well. Serve at room temperature.

SERVES 2.

Wild Mushroom and Juniper Berry Sandwiches

In Provence in the fall, locals scour the woods with baskets for chanterelles and other wild mushrooms. The earthiness of mushrooms marries well with the distinctive pungency of juniper.

LE GENIÈVRE

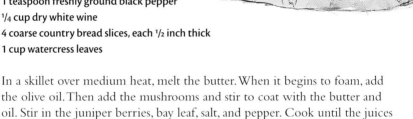

¹/₂ teaspoon unsalted butter
1 teaspoon olive oil
¹/₂ pound chanterelle or oyster mushrooms
3 juniper berries, bruised
1 bay leaf
¹/₂ teaspoon salt
1 teaspoon freshly ground black pepper
¹/₄ cup dry white wine
4 coarse country bread slices, each ¹/₂ inch thick
1 cup watercress leaves

In a skillet over medium heat, melt the butter. When it begins to foam, add the olive oil. Then add the mushrooms and stir to coat with the butter and oil. Stir in the juniper berries, bay leaf, salt, and pepper. Cook until the juices from the mushrooms are released, about 3 minutes. Add the white wine and stir to disperse the ingredients, reduce the heat to low, cover, and simmer until the mushrooms are very soft and the juice has thickened slightly, about 20 minutes. Remove from the heat and discard the bay leaf.

Cut bread slices in half and place two halves on each individual plate. Top each with equal portions of the watercress leaves and then with equal portions of the mushroom mixture. Serve immediately.

SERVES 4.

Dried Herbes de Provence Blends

Potato Soup

Potato Salad with Herbes de Provence

Niçoise-Style Salad

Lamb and Tomatoes with Polenta

Grilled Lamb Chops

Grilled Vegetables

Crispy Roasted Potatoes

Summer Squashes with White Wine

Gratin of Fennel, Gruyère, and Parmesan

Socca Crêpes with Herbes de Provence

Provençal-Style Fish Soup

Soup with Pistou

Artichokes Braised with Tomatoes

Dried Herbes de Provence Blends

Fresh herbs can easily be dried at home for making your own herbes de Provence blends. Make sure the herbs are clean and dry, as any moisture will cause mold to grow. You will need a long-handled wooden spoon; kitchen string; small jars, lock-top plastic bags, or other airtight containers; and labels.

Create small bunches of individual herbs and, using ten-inch lengths of string, tightly bind each bunch at the stem ends, leaving at least four inches of string dangling from either side of the knot. Tie the first bunch of herbs to the base of the spoon handle where the bowl begins, with the stem ends pointing up the handle and the herbs resting on the bowl. Tie the second bunch so that the leafy portion just covers the stem ends of the already-attached bunch. Continue in this manner, marching the bunches up the handle. Then hang or prop up the spoon, handle pointing upward, in a dry area out of direct sunlight. The herbs will dry fully in seven to ten days; the timing will depend upon the humidity.

In place of the spoon, you can use a long wooden dowel about $1/4$ inch in diameter, suspending it horizontally from a wall or cupboard on screw hooks and hanging the tied bunches as if they were clothes drying on a line. You can also use a basket lined with a dish towel, spreading the herbs in loose piles and overlapping them only slightly.

If you wish to dry orange or lemon zest in the basket along with the herbs, use a sharp paring knife to remove the zest from the fruit, beginning at the stem end and working downward. Create a singular ribbon about $1/2$ inch wide and be careful to cut away only the colored part of the peel, to avoid the bitterness carried in the white pith.

Once the herbs are thoroughly dry, you can begin to make your herbes de Provence mixtures. The texture of a mix is just as important as the individual ingredients. Begin by removing all the leaves from the woody stems and discarding the stems. Using your fingers, gently crumble the larger leaves to a fine consistency. Do not grind them to a powder. Smaller leaves, such as those of thyme and winter savory, can be left whole, although rubbing them breaks their surfaces and helps to release their flavor. Rosemary leaves should be dried whole, then minced before using. Mix the herbs as you like and then store the mixtures in labeled jars or other airtight containers. Or you can keep the crumbled herbs separate in order to make custom mixtures as you cook. In either case, store the herbs in a cool, dark place for up to three months. At that point, toss out the herbs and start again. Although they will not have gone bad, their flavors will have faded.

Herbes de Provence Blends

The following dried herb mixtures include one classic, which joins thyme, rosemary, bay, and fennel. This combination can be used as a base, adding or substituting other herbs as you like. Also included are two favorite mixtures of mine that are less conventional because they incorporate lavender, mint, lemon thyme, and citrus zest. The combinations can be made ahead of time, which allows the various flavors to infuse together. When mixing with bay, leave the bay leaves whole and make the combination ahead of time, allowing the bay to infuse the other herbs.

HERBES DE PROVENCE BLEND I ~ Use this classic mixture for meat, fish, and vegetables.

2 tablespoons dried thyme
2 tablespoons dried rosemary
2 bay leaves
1 teaspoon fennel seeds

HERBES DE PROVENCE BLEND II ~ Use this mixture for pork, beef, and wild game or fowl.

2 tablespoons dried thyme
2 tablespoons crumbled dried sage
1/2 teaspoon crumbled dried lavender leaves
   or 1 teaspoon crumbled dried mint
2 bay leaves
2-inch piece dried orange zest

HERBES DE PROVENCE BLEND III ~ Use this mixture for fish, poultry, and vegetables.

1 teaspoon fennel seeds
2 tablespoons dried winter savory
1 teaspoon dried rosemary
1 teaspoon dried lemon thyme
2-inch piece dried lemon zest

Potato Soup

This hearty potato soup is seasoned with dried herbs and with smoky bacon, which in France is bought as meaty chunks of lardon.

2 thick slices bacon, cut crosswise into ¼-inch-thick pieces
1 yellow onion, finely chopped
1 carrot, peeled and finely chopped
1 stalk celery, finely chopped
2 teaspoons herbes de Provence
½ teaspoon salt
1 teaspoon freshly ground black pepper
4 cups vegetable or chicken stock
2 pounds white- or yellow-fleshed potatoes,
    peeled and cut into medium dice
2 tablespoons snipped (or minced) fresh chives

In a large saucepan over medium heat, fry the bacon until its fat is released, just a few minutes. Add the onion, carrot, celery, herbs, salt, and pepper; cook, stirring often, until the mixture is soft, 6 to 7 minutes. Add the stock and bring to a boil. Add the potatoes, return to a boil, stirring often, and cook for 2 to 3 minutes. Reduce to a simmer and cook, uncovered, until potatoes are tender and can easily be pierced with a fork, 10 to 15 minutes.

To serve, ladle into warmed bowls and garnish with the chives.

SERVES 4.

Potato Salad with Herbes de Provence

A refreshing change from deli potato salad, this version is held together with aïoli, the garlic mayonnaise of Provence.

3 quarts water
1 1/4 teaspoons salt
2 pounds new potatoes,
   halved or quartered
6 green onions, including about two inches
   of green tops, finely chopped
1 red bell pepper, seeded,
   deribbed, and finely diced
1 teaspoon freshly ground black pepper
2 teaspoons herbes de Provence
   (see page 46)

FOR THE GARLIC MAYONNAISE:
2 cloves garlic, peeled
1/4 teaspoon salt
2 egg yolks, at room temperature
1 cup olive oil

In a saucepan, bring the water to a boil. Add 1 teaspoon of the salt and the potatoes and boil until tender but not mushy, 10 to 15 minutes. Drain into a colander and set aside to cool.

TO MAKE THE GARLIC MAYONNAISE: Finely crush together the garlic and salt in a small bowl or mortar. In another small bowl, whisk the egg yolks until they are pale yellow. Then add the olive oil a few drops at a time while whisking continuously. Be careful not to add too much oil at once, as this will prevent the mayonnaise from setting. Once the mixture has emulsified, the oil can be added in a slow, steady drizzle. When all of the oil has been incorporated, stir in the garlic-salt mixture.

Transfer the cooled potatoes to a large salad bowl. Gently stir in the remaining 1/4 teaspoon salt, the green onions, bell pepper, black pepper, and herbs. Finally, stir in the mayonnaise just until the potatoes are evenly coated. Serve chilled or at room temperature.

SERVES 8.

Niçoise-Style Salad

In this contemporary version of a Provençal classic, seared fresh tuna is used instead of canned, and the anchovy is blended into the dressing.

FOR THE VINAIGRETTE:
1 clove garlic, peeled
1 anchovy fillet
1 teaspoon red wine vinegar
½ teaspoon Dijon mustard
1 tablespoon extra-virgin
    olive oil

FOR THE FISH AND SALAD:
⅓ cup herbes de Provence (see page 46)
½ teaspoon salt
1 pound ahi tuna fillet, about 1½ inches thick,
    cut into 4 equal pieces
2 tablespoons corn or peanut oil
½ pound mixed baby greens
12 salt-cured black olives
12 cherry tomatoes such as Sweet 100s or Sungold
2 eggs, hard-boiled, peeled, and thinly sliced crosswise
2 teaspoons capers

TO MAKE THE VINAIGRETTE: In the bottom of a bowl, mash together the garlic and anchovy fillet. Whisk in the vinegar and mustard and drizzle in the olive oil until incorporated.

FOR THE FISH AND SALAD: Spread the herbs and salt on a small plate. Roll the tuna pieces in the herbs to coat on all sides. Place a large nonstick skillet over high heat and add the vegetable oil. As soon as the oil begins to smoke, carefully lay the tuna pieces in the skillet. Cook, pressing down gently with a spatula, until seared on the first side, about 2 minutes, then turn and cook for 2 minutes longer again pressing gently with spatula. If you prefer your tuna more fully cooked, reduce the heat slightly and cook a little longer on each side until opaque throughout. Set aside.

Add the salad greens to the vinaigrette and toss. Divide the greens among 4 individual plates. Place a piece of tuna atop each pile of greens. Garnish with the olives, tomatoes, egg slices, and capers. Serve at once.

SERVES 4.

Lamb and Tomatoes with Polenta

An English friend makes shepherd's pie each time she visits me. This deep-dish polenta-and-lamb casserole was inspired by her signature dish.

1 pound ground lamb
1 green bell pepper, seeded, deribbed, and diced
2 shallots, finely chopped
2 cloves garlic, peeled and coarsely chopped
1 tablespoon herbes de Provence (see page 46)
1 bay leaf
$^1/_2$ teaspoon salt
1 teaspoon freshly ground black pepper
1 pound ripe tomatoes, seeded and coarsely chopped,
    or 1 large can stewed tomatoes, drained and
    coarsely chopped
1 teaspoon unsalted butter, cut into bits

FOR THE POLENTA:
2 $^1/_4$ cups water
1 teaspoon salt
1 teaspoon unsalted butter
$^1/_2$ cup polenta
$^1/_4$ cup freshly grated Parmesan cheese

Preheat an oven to 450 degrees F.

Heat a large nonstick skillet over medium heat and crumble in the ground lamb. Cook, turning often, until lightly browned, 5 to 7 minutes. Discard excess fat, and add the bell pepper, shallots, garlic, herbs, bay leaf, and salt and pepper. Sauté until the bell pepper is soft and the meat is cooked through, about 10 minutes. Stir in the tomatoes and reduce the heat to low. Cook, stirring occasionally, until the sauce has thickened, another 15 to 20 minutes.

MEANWHILE, PREPARE THE POLENTA: In a saucepan, bring the water to a rolling boil. Add the salt and 1 teaspoon butter. Slowly whisk in the polenta. It is important to stir constantly so no lumps form. Continue to cook over high heat, stirring constantly, until the water is fully absorbed, about 5 minutes. Reduce the heat to low and cook for another 15 minutes, continuing to stir constantly. The polenta should be thick and creamy. Remove from heat and let stand for 5 to 10 minutes.

Transfer the lamb mixture to a baking dish at least 3 inches deep. Spread the polenta evenly over the top, covering the lamb mixture completely. Sprinkle the surface with the Parmesan and dot with the butter. Bake until the juices are bubbling and the polenta has seeped into the lamb, 15 to 20 minutes. Serve immediately straight from the baking dish.

SERVES 6.

Grilled Lamb Chops

It is preferable to grill these tiny chops over a charcoal fire, but slipping them under a broiler will do. Accompany with a simple tomato-basil salad.

1/4 cup herbes de Provence (see page 46)
4 cloves garlic, peeled and minced
1 teaspoon salt
1 teaspoon freshly ground black pepper
12 small lamb rib chops

In a small bowl, combine the herbs, garlic, salt, and pepper. Rub the herb mixture into both sides of the lamb chops and wrap them together in plastic wrap. Refrigerate for at least 1 hour or for up to 24 hours.

Prepare a fire in a charcoal grill or preheat a broiler. Cook the lamb chops on the grill or in the broiler, turning once, for 3 to 4 minutes on each side for medium rare or until done to your liking. Serve immediately.

SERVES 4.

Grilled Vegetables

Cook up a batch of these vegetables on Saturday morning, and use them over the weekend for sandwiches, pasta sauces, and omelets.

3 tablespoons olive oil
Juice of 1 lemon
1 teaspoon balsamic vinegar
1 clove garlic, peeled and crushed
2 teaspoons herbes de Provence (see page 46)
¹/₂ teaspoon salt
2 yellow bell peppers, seeded, deribbed, and
    cut lengthwise into 1-inch-wide strips
2 red bell peppers, seeded, deribbed, and
    cut lengthwise into 1-inch-wide strips
4 Japanese eggplants, ends trimmed and
    cut lengthwise into ¹/₂-inch-thick slices
10 to 12 asparagus spears, tough ends removed
6 green onions or green garlics, root ends and
    tough greens trimmed

Prepare a charcoal fire in a grill or preheat a broiler.

In a large bowl, stir together the olive oil, lemon juice, vinegar, garlic, herbs, and salt. Add all the vegetables and toss to coat well. Cover and let stand for 15 minutes.

Lift the vegetables from the marinade with tongs and arrange in a hinged grill basket or on a broiler pan. Grill or broil, turning as needed, until cooked through and just beginning to crisp and blacken on the edges, 7 to 8 minutes. Serve hot or at room temperature.

SERVES 4.

Crispy Roasted Potatoes

These small, crispy potatoes are smothered in the Provençal flavors of fruity olive oil, garlic, and fragrant herbs.

2 pounds mixed new potatoes such as Red Rose
    and Yellow Finn, halved
3 tablespoons extra-virgin olive oil
4 cloves garlic, peeled and bruised but left whole
1 tablespoon herbes de Provence (see page 46)
1 teaspoon freshly ground black pepper
$1/2$ teaspoon salt

Preheat an oven to 450 degrees F.

Place the potatoes in a large bowl. Drizzle the olive oil over them. Using your hands or a wooden spoon, turn the potatoes until they are thoroughly coated with the oil. Transfer the potatoes to a baking sheet, spreading them out in a single layer, and scatter the garlic cloves over the top. Sprinkle the potatoes with the herbs, pepper, and salt.

Bake, turning with a spatula every 20 minutes or so, until crispy and golden, about 1 hour. Serve hot.

SERVES 4 TO 6.

Summer Squashes with White Wine
A perfect side dish to help use up the bounty of squashes in your backyard garden.

3 teaspoons extra-virgin olive oil
1 clove garlic, peeled and crushed
2 pounds mixed baby summer squashes such as
    pattypan, crookneck, or Ronde de Nice,
    trimmed and halved or quartered
2 teaspoons herbes de Provence (see page 46)
1 teaspoon freshly ground black pepper
$^1/_2$ teaspoon salt
$^1/_2$ cup dry white wine

Preheat an oven to 375 degrees F.

Using 1 teaspoon of the olive oil, brush the bottom and sides of a baking dish with a lid. Then rub the oiled surfaces with the crushed garlic. Discard the garlic.

Place the squashes in the baking dish and drizzle with the remaining 2 teaspoons olive oil. Turn the squashes in the dish to coat well with the oil. Sprinkle evenly with the herbs, pepper, and salt.

Bake, uncovered, for 10 minutes. Add the white wine to the dish and cover with the lid. Continue to cook until the squashes are easily pierced with a fork, about 30 minutes. Serve hot.

SERVES 4.

Gratin of Fennel, Gruyère, and Parmesan

In this dish, sweet fennel is layered with a pair of cheeses and baked until a bubbling, golden brown crust forms on the top.

1 clove garlic, peeled and crushed
4 large fennel bulbs
2 teaspoons herbes de Provence (see page 46)
$^1/_2$ teaspoon red pepper flakes
$^1/_4$ teaspoon salt
1 teaspoon freshly ground black pepper
$^1/_4$ cup freshly grated Gruyère cheese
$^1/_4$ cup freshly grated Parmesan cheese
$^1/_2$ cup vegetable or chicken stock
$^1/_4$ cup coarse dried bread crumbs, preferably
    from a baguette or coarse country loaf
1 teaspoon unsalted butter, cut into bits

Preheat an oven to 425 degrees F.

Select an 8-by-8-inch baking dish and rub the bottom and sides with the crushed garlic. Discard the garlic.

Cut off the stems and feathery tops from the fennel bulbs and trim away any bruised or otherwise damaged stalks. Cut away the tough cores and cut crosswise into $^1/_4$-inch-thick slices.

Using about one-fourth of the fennel slices, form a layer in the bottom of the dish, covering it completely. Lightly sprinkle with about one-fourth of

each of the herbs, red pepper flakes, salt, black pepper, Gruyère, and Parmesan. Repeat the layers until the dish is full, ending with the cheeses. You should have three to four layers of fennel. Pour in the stock around the edges of the dish, then evenly sprinkle the top with the bread crumbs. Dot with the butter.

Bake until the gratin is bubbling around the edges and the top is golden brown, about 30 to 40 minutes. Serve hot directly from the dish.

SERVES 6.

Socca Crêpes with Herbes de Provence

Golden brown, buttery socca, a crisp, thin snack made from chickpea flour, is baked in woodfired ovens and sold on the streets of Nice. These crêpes are a delicious at-home variation.

2 cups chickpea flour
1 ½ cups water
1 egg, well beaten
1 tablespoon extra virgin olive oil
1 tablespoon herbes de Provence (see page 46)
1 teaspoon salt
Butter for cooking crêpes

In a large bowl, whisk together chickpea flour, water, egg, olive oil, herbs, and salt.

In an 8- to 10-inch non-stick skillet, melt about ½ teaspoon of butter over medium heat. Pour in ⅓ cup of the batter and swirl pan to evenly coat the bottom. Cook until the edges begin to crisp and the center is opaque, about 1 minute. Turn over and cook another 40 seconds or so. Repeat the process, adding butter as needed. Serve piping hot with plenty of butter. Makes 8 to 10 crêpes.

SERVES 4 TO 5.

Provençal-Style Fish Soup

At least once each summer when I was a child, my family would go fishing, either off the coastal cliffs of Northern California or the riverbanks of Provence. Since our efforts did not usually bring us large, delectable catches, what we hooked nearly always went into making this soup. It incorporates different types of fish and includes frames, tails, and even heads, for flavor. Serve with grilled coarse country bread rubbed with garlic and drizzled with olive oil.

2 tablespoons light vegetable oil

2 yellow onions, coarsely chopped

1 tablespoon herbes de Provence (see page 46)

2 bay leaves

3 pounds mixed fish such as snapper, halibut, trout, and bass,
    cleaned and cut up, including frames, tails, and heads

6 cloves garlic, peeled but left whole

2 stalks celery, cut into 1-inch pieces

2 carrots, peeled and cut into 1/2-inch-thick rounds

3/4 pound ripe tomatoes, quartered

1 small fennel bulb, core and any bruised stalks removed
    and bulb quartered

2 tablespoons tomato paste

2 cups dry white wine

4 cups vegetable or chicken stock

1/2 teaspoon salt

1 teaspoon freshly ground black pepper

In a large saucepan over medium heat, warm the oil. Add the onions, herbes de Provence, and bay leaves and sauté, stirring often, until the onions are translucent and just begin to brown, about 7 minutes. Add the fish and brown on all sides, about 5 minutes longer. Add the garlic, celery, carrots, tomatoes, and fennel. Cook, stirring often to prevent sticking, until the vegetables soften slightly, another 5 to 7 minutes. Stir in the tomato paste and as soon as it begins to stick, pour in the white wine. Deglaze the pan, stirring vigorously to loosen any browned bits that may be stuck to the sides and bottom. Add the stock, raise the heat to high, and bring to a boil. Reduce the heat to low and add salt and pepper. Simmer, uncovered, for 1 hour to blend the flavors fully.

Remove from the heat and let cool slightly. Scoop out and discard any visible bones. Working in batches, purée the soup in a food processor or blender. Strain the soup through a fine-mesh sieve, pushing against the solids with a wooden spoon in order to extract as much flavor as possible.

Return the soup to a clean saucepan over medium heat and taste and adjust the seasonings. Reheat to serving temperature, adding a little water if the soup is too thick. Ladle into warmed bowls and serve at once.

SERVES 6.

Soup with Pistou

Pistou is the Provençal sister to Italian pesto. A generous spoonful is stirred into individual servings of this summery vegetable soup.

2 tablespoons olive oil

1 red onion, finely chopped

2 cloves garlic, peeled and minced

2 pounds ripe tomatoes, diced

3 yellow-fleshed potatoes such as Yukon Gold,
    peeled and cut into $^1/_2$-inch dice

$^1/_4$ pound snap beans such as Blue Lake or Yellow Wax

1 cup shelling beans such as cranberry or flageolet
    (about $^2/_3$ pound unshelled)

1 tablespoon herbes de Provence (see page 46)

8 cups vegetable or chicken stock

$^1/_2$ teaspoon salt

1-inch square rind from Parmesan or other hard cheese

$^1/_2$ cup broken dried vermicelli noodles (1-inch pieces)

FOR THE PISTOU:

4 cloves garlic, peeled

$^1/_2$ teaspoon salt

2 cups fresh basil leaves

$^1/_4$ cup olive oil

$^1/_4$ cup freshly grated Parmesan cheese

In a large soup pot over medium heat, warm the olive oil. Add the onion and sauté, stirring occasionally, until browned, about 7 minutes. Stir in the garlic and tomatoes and cook, stirring occasionally, until the tomatoes begin to release their liquid, about 5 minutes. Add the potatoes, snap beans, shelling beans, and herbs and continue to cook over medium heat, stirring often, for another 5 minutes. Add the stock, salt, and cheese rind, raise the heat to high, and bring to a boil. Reduce the heat to low and cook, uncovered, until the beans and potatoes are nearly tender, about 15 minutes. Add the vermicelli and cook until tender, about 10 minutes longer.

MEANWHILE, MAKE THE PISTOU: This can be done by hand in a bowl or mortar or in a blender or food processor. Crush or process the garlic and salt together, then add the basil leaves and mash or process to create a paste. If using a blender or processor, have the motor running and slowly drizzle in the olive oil. If making by hand, add the oil slowly while whisking constantly.

To serve, remove and discard the cheese rind. Ladle the soup into warmed bowls and stir in 1 tablespoon of the pistou into each bowl. Sprinkle with the Parmesan and pass the remaining pistou at the table.

SERVES 6.

Artichokes Braised with Tomatoes

This traditional Provençal dish, known as artichaut à la barigoule, *calls for slowly cooking small artichokes in a thick, tomatoey sauce. Serve with warm grilled baguette slices and a green salad.*

12 baby artichokes, the size of large eggs
3 tablespoons olive oil
1 yellow onion, thinly sliced
1 tablespoon herbes de Provence (see page 46)
2 cloves garlic, peeled and coarsely chopped
1 pound ripe tomatoes, coarsely chopped
2 carrots, peeled, quartered lengthwise, and
   then cut crosswise into 1-inch pieces
2 cups dry white wine
¼ cup vegetable or chicken stock

Preheat an oven to 350 degrees F.

Remove the tough outer leaves of the artichokes, then cut off the spiky leaf tips and trim the stems even with the bottoms.

In a large skillet or flameproof baking dish with a tight-fitting lid, warm the olive oil over high heat. Add the onion and sauté, stirring often, until lightly browned, about 5 minutes. Add the herbs and the garlic and cook for another 30 to 40 seconds. Stir in the tomatoes and carrots and cook for 3 to 4 minutes. Place the artichokes, stem ends down, in the skillet or dish and add the wine and stock. Cover with the lid and transfer to the oven. Bake until the artichokes are tender and the inner leaves can easily be pulled out, about 1 hour. Serve hot.

SERVES 4.

LIQUID AND DRY MEASURES

U.S.	METRIC
1/4 teaspoon	1.25 milliliters
1/2 teaspoon	2.5 milliliters
1 teaspoon	5 milliliters
1 tablespoon (3 teaspoons)	15 milliliters
1 fluid ounce (2 tablespoons)	30 milliliters
1/4 cup	60 milliliters
1/3 cup	80 milliliters
1 cup	240 milliliters
1 pint (2 cups)	480 milliliters
1 quart (4 cups, 32 ounces)	960 milliliters
1 gallon (4 quarts)	3.84 liters
1 ounce (by weight)	28 grams
1 pound	454 grams
2.2 pounds	1 kilogram

LENGTH MEASURES

U.S.	METRIC
1/8 inch	3 millimeters
1/4 inch	6 millimeters
1/2 inch	12 millimeters
1 inch	2.5 centimeters

OVEN TEMPERATURES

FAHRENHEIT	CELSIUS	GAS
250	120	1/2
275	140	1
300	150	2
325	160	3
350	180	4
375	190	5
400	200	6
425	220	7
450	230	8
475	240	9
500	260	10